THE PALAC HOLYROODHoUSE

FROM ABBEY TO PALACE

The Palace of Holyroodhouse has its origins in an Augustinian monastery founded on the site by David I in 1128. This abbey probably took its name from its most precious relic, a fragment of the True Cross brought to Scotland by the King's mother, St Margaret. According to medieval legend, the King founded his abbey on the spot where, while hunting, he had a vision of a stag with a cross between its antlers. The symbol of the Abbey, and its successor the Palace, is therefore a stag's head with the horns framing a cross.

The Abbey prospered and devoted its wealth to an ambitious architectural programme at the turn of the twelfth century. As Edinburgh became recognized as Scotland's capital, her kings preferred to establish their quarters in the Abbey, surrounded by its park, rather than in the Castle, exposed to the elements on its rock. The Abbey thus became the setting for many events in Scotland's history. By degrees the Palace buildings eclipsed the Abbey. James IV made additions in anticipation of his marriage to Margaret Tudor, celebrated in the Abbey in 1503, but only the fragmentary trace of his gatehouse, wantonly destroyed in 1753, survives. His successor James V has left a more substantial monument in the massive Tower constructed between 1528 and 1532. Between 1535 and 1536, the King embarked on a second building campaign to create the west front south of the Royal Apartment in his

ABOVE: *Heraldic panel on the Abbey Church wall*
BELOW: *West front of the Palace*

tower. With its great expanses of glazing and ornamental crestings, this addition, domestic rather than defensive, may have been begun in anticipation of the King's first marriage. His second wife, Mary of Guise, was crowned in the Abbey.

Their daughter, the Catholic Mary Queen of Scots, returned to a Protestant Scotland after the death of her husband Francis II, King of France. Many of the dramatic events of her short reign took place in the Abbey and Palace of Holyroohouse, including her marriage to Lord Darnley, the murder of her secretary Rizzio and her later marriage to the Earl of Bothwell. No Scottish monarch was to be more closely associated with Holyroodhouse than Mary Queen of Scots and it became a shrine to her cult.

Although her son James VI held his councils here, his succession to the English throne in 1603 led to an inevitable dimming of the Palace's glories. It was renovated for his return in 1617 and in 1633 for the Scottish coronation of his son, Charles I. In the Cromwellian Wars the Palace was damaged, then repaired by Cromwell's troops.

THE REBUILDING BY CHARLES II

After his restoration in 1660, Charles II was crowned in Scotland. Although he never returned he took pains to have the Palace restored. The combined talents of his Secretary of State for Scotland, the

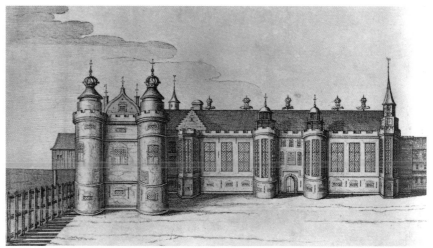

TOP: *The Palace in c. 1544, from the English Spy Map*
ABOVE: *The Palace in c. 1650 after Gordon of Rothiemay*

Duke of Lauderdale, who directed the work, the King's Surveyor of Royal Works, Sir William Bruce, and Robert Mylne, the King's Master Mason, ensured that Holyroodhouse emerged as the key monument in the history of Scottish classical architecture.

Bruce's design employed the Orders of Architecture with a grammatical correctness new to Scotland, while Lauderdale's sumptuous interiors, with their fine plasterwork, carving and decorative

painting blended into a baroque unity, to be widely copied in Scotland. The King, who insisted on practicality, required only a single new Royal Apartment to the east, while the old Royal Apartment in James V's Tower was to be patched up and subsequently assigned to the Queen. The Abbey Church was to be made into the Chapel Royal. The second floor was to provide accommodation for the court during the King's residence, and in his absence for the officers of state.

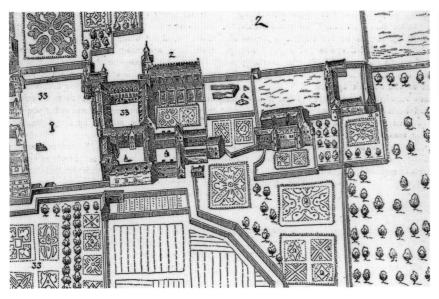

The Palace in 1647 after Gordon of Rothiemay

The success of Bruce's design was the result of a deliberate continuity with the earlier buildings. James V's Tower established the height of the ranges around the principal court. The Tower was duplicated across the west front for symmetry. The new rooms were arranged around the court, which was articulated by superimposed Doric, Ionic and Corinthian pilasters. The open piazzas on the ground floor perhaps recalled the Palace's monastic origins. By 1676, it was resolved to take down the west front, which had not been improved by an extra storey added by Cromwell. It was rebuilt in ashlar with a Doric frontispiece. James V's fortress-like Tower was tamed into domesticity with the removal of the iron grilles protecting its windows which were now sashed.

The quality of the interior was the result of Lauderdale's ability to lure north a team of craftsmen, who introduced Scotland to a new style.

One of the glories of the Palace is the range of virtuoso fretwork ceilings by the English plasterers, John Houlbert and George Dunsterfield. The other artists were Dutch. Alexander Eizat panelled the rooms in a style which blended Dutch Palladianism with the decoration of Louis Quatorze. Jan van Santvoort was responsible for sculptural enrichments no less vigorous than the plaster ceilings. Jacob de Wet was engaged to carry out a programme of decorative painting. Their contributions created a stylistic unity in the few rooms that were to be completely realized, such as the King's Bedchamber.

JAMES VII

The new Palace provided a suitably private residence in 1679 for the King's Catholic brother, James, Duke of York. When he succeeded as James VII in 1685, the new King commanded that the Chapel Royal be fitted up for Catholic ritual and the ceremonies of the Order of the Thistle, Scotland's ancient Order of chivalry. Until this could be realized, the Council Chamber, in the new south-west tower, was to serve as the temporary Chapel Royal.

Altar plate was commissioned in London and sent north and Bruce designed classical stalls for the Knights of the Thistle. A Jesuit college was established in the Palace precincts. Before the Chapel Royal was finished, James VII had been forced to flee the country and his daughter Mary and son-in-law William of Orange had ascended the throne. A riotous mob marched on the Palace and destroyed every vestige of Catholicism – but David Burnet, one of the priests, spirited away the most portable elements of the altar plate to the north-east, where they were preserved by the Catholic mission there.

Although the Palace lacked a court, the great officers of state were given apartments on the second floor. There they indulged the Scottish love of display in their costly equipages and state beds. After the Union of Parliaments in 1707 much of this splendour was redirected to Scotland's castles and country houses. Because no king came, still less a queen, the Duke and Duchess of Hamilton, who had been created Hereditary Keepers of the Palace by Charles I, appropriated the Queen's apartments and furnished them sumptuously.

THE EIGHTEENTH CENTURY

After the departure of the Scottish Parliament, the Young Pretender (Bonnie Prince Charlie) held court there in 1745, followed by the Duke of Cumberland, commander of the Hanoverian troops who suppressed the 1745 Jacobite Rebellion.

The collapse of the roof of the Abbey Church in 1768, after ineffectual repairs in 1758, left the Chapel Royal in ruins. The failure to rebuild the Abbey was symbolic of a loss of national pride. Similarly, portraits in the Picture Gallery mutilated by English troops remained on display unrepaired for many years. This air of neglect, however, was to foster the development of the Palace as the prime Scottish tourist attraction when the romantic fascination with Mary Queen of Scots' doomed reign began to cast its spell. The attention of visitors now shifted from Charles II's relatively modern baroque Palace to the old Royal Apartments in James V's Tower.

THE FRENCH PRINCES

In 1795 the Royal Apartment was offered to the Comte d'Artois, brother of Louis XVI of France, in exile with his family. A compelling attraction for the Prince was the sanctuary it traditionally offered to debtors, provided they remained within the Abbey precincts on weekdays. The Scottish Catholic Church returned the surviving pieces of James VII's altar plate to the Palace so that it could be used once more in the Catholic chapel which was established in the Great Gallery. Charles II's suite was fitted up for him by the Edinburgh furniture makers, Young, Trotter and Hamilton. The handsome Edinburgh New Town furniture they supplied for the Prince in 1796 was reissued when he returned to the Palace as the deposed King Charles X of France, and has continued in general use as the primary furnishing stock of the Palace to the present day.

KING GEORGE IV'S STATE VISIT TO SCOTLAND

In 1822 George IV made his state visit to Scotland. As Holyroodhouse was not thought to be a suitable residence for a monarch with such luxurious tastes, he lodged at the Duke of Buccleuch's seat, Dalkeith Palace, but Holyroodhouse was spruced up to serve as a setting for the King's drawing rooms and levees, at which the King donned Highland dress in honour of his Scottish subjects. The new furniture provided for the occasion was merely hired from Trotter's and left shortly after the King. George IV's visit placed a spotlight on the Palace, swelling the number of visitors and leading to money being voted for improvements. The King's architect in Scotland, Sir Robert Reid, cleared away the sprawl of buildings that clung to Bruce's Palace, leaving it four-square and sheathed in an envelope of polished ashlar. The King commanded that Mary Queen of Scots' apartments should be 'preserved sacred from every alteration'.

The Chapel Royal as altered for the Knights of the Thistle by James VII

An important consequence of these repairs was William IV's decision in 1834 to permit his Commissioner to the General Assembly of the Church of Scotland to reside in the Palace during the annual meeting of the General Assembly.

QUEEN VICTORIA AT HOLYROODHOUSE

In 1842 Queen Victoria made a state visit to Scotland. Like George IV, she resided at Dalkeith Palace. Although, as a result of a last-minute outbreak of scarlet fever, she did not visit the Palace her delight in Scotland was to inspire her to acquire Balmoral Castle in Aberdeenshire in 1848 as her Highland holiday home.

The Palace of Holyroodhouse was identified as a strategically placed stop on the journey north to Balmoral. For the Scots, the Queen's return in 1850 to the Palace of her Stuart ancestors was seen as an event of deep emotive significance. By degrees Holyroodhouse was reinstated as Scotland's premier royal residence. Because there were grace-and-favour tenants, the Royal Family had to endure the discomfort of Charles II's Royal Apartment, although this was beginning to acquire an antiquarian charm.

The renovations were supervised from London, but the Office of Works' Scottish architect, Robert Matheson, championed its cause in the face of the Treasury's cheeseparing economy. He stretched funds by appealing to the goodwill of Edinburgh's tradesmen, who took London's financial stringency as a national slight against the Scots. Trotter's firm stripped Charles II's oak panelling of its later disfiguring white paint and the interior decorator D. R. Hay cleaned the spectacular plaster ceilings and repainted them in rich colours. The tenants' furniture, combined with that supplied for the French Princes, was enriched with pieces from Buckingham Palace. In 1856 the Throne Room was given an antiquarian heraldic ceiling. Matheson also did much to improve the Palace's immediate surroundings.

Now that the Palace was the centre of attention, the Lord Provost

Sir David Wilkie: The Entrance of George IV at Holyroodhouse

George Greig: The Queen's Bedroom, Holyroodhouse, 1863 *(now the King's Ante-Chamber)*

of Edinburgh applied pressure to increase public access. In 1852 the Duke of Hamilton released his rooms in James V's Tower. In 1855 the Office of Works appointed staff to show 'the Historical Apartments': the Great Gallery, Mary Queen of Scots' Rooms (tours of which had previously been led by the Duke's servants) and the first-floor Tower rooms (vacated by the Duke), which became known as the 'Darnley Rooms'.

EDWARD VII
When Prince of Wales, Edward VII had lived in the Palace while being tutored by masters of the Royal High School in 1859. Although Queen Victoria's return had transformed the Palace's fortunes, it still suffered from its classification as a 'temporary residence', and a failure to invest in more than running repairs meant that its drains were deemed in no state to receive him in 1903, so he was obliged to lodge at Dalkeith Palace.

Edwardian enthusiasm for period furniture styles prompted the restoration of Mary Queen of Scots' rooms, which had been left to deteriorate. The 'Darnley bed' and some of the chairs were restored by the Royal School of Needlework and the tables restored by Whytock and Reid, the Edinburgh furniture makers. Although these repairs were seen as an improvement, the atmosphere of decay that had made the rooms so visually seductive was lost.

The blank panels on James V's Tower were filled with new armorial carvings: a unicorn copied from a surviving fragment and the arms of Mary of Guise.

KING GEORGE V AND QUEEN MARY
It was thus left to King George V and Queen Mary to adapt the Palace to the needs of the twentieth century. Before their state visit in 1911, a number of changes were made, including the repanelling of Charles

II's Council Chamber. There was so little accommodation for their court that temporary buildings had to be erected in the grounds. By degrees surrounding buildings were adapted and under the supervision of their Scottish architects in the Office of Works, the essential modern services including bathrooms, electric light and lifts were introduced unobtrusively. The public tour was extended to embrace Charles II's state rooms. Playing-up the Carolean character of the Palace has tended to be at the expense of any surviving remnants of Victorian decorations.

QUEEN ELIZABETH II
The smooth running of the Palace today owes much to Charles II's foresight in providing a spacious upper floor where the Royal Family's private apartments are now situated. The Queen's annual visit is usually in the last week of June or the first week in July but Holyroodhouse also bursts into life with ceremony in the third week of May, when the Lord High Commissioner to the General Assembly of the Church of Scotland holds court. Many Scots from all areas of national life are entertained at garden parties and receptions. The Palace has never been so intensively used as it is today. Members of the Royal Family stay frequently while carrying out engagements in Scotland. More of the Palace and its gardens are open to visitors than at any time in its history.

VISITORS ARE received in the newly restored and adapted Guardhouse, designed by Robert Matheson in the baronial style and completed in 1861. Although the entrance front of the Palace appears to be a uniform symmetrical composition, the greater antiquity of James V's Tower of 1528-32 to the left is apparent in its battered stonework and the scars where iron grilles were removed from its windows in 1676. By contrast, Bruce's balancing right-hand tower of 1671 has the regularity of a pasteboard toy fort. Although the foundations of the central connecting block incorporate those of James V's extensions to his Tower of 1534-5, the early work was taken down in 1676 and rebuilt in classical style. The central doorway of the Palace was conceived as a triumphal gateway framed by Doric columns and surmounted by the royal arms, carved to a design by Jacob de Wet in 1677, under a crowned cupola rising behind the broken pediment. Because the west front is so much lower than the flanking towers, the symmetrical façades of the inner court, articulated by correctly detailed classical pilasters, can be glimpsed behind, contrasting with James V's massive fortified Tower.

In 1858, to give a more ornamental character to the Forecourt, Matheson designed the decorative fountain in the centre, taking the early seventeenth-century fountain

ABOVE AND BELOW: *State visit of the King of Norway 1994*

at Linlithgow as his model. To the right of the Guardhouse gateway a richly detailed but now weather-worn doorway topped by a thistle has been set in the wall. This was salvaged from the stone walls of the Privy Garden to the north of the Forecourt which had been demolished in 1856 when the carriageway to the Palace was rerouted to avoid Canongate: as fashionable Edinburgh had moved to the New Town, it had degenerated from an aristocratic quarter into Victorian slums, and was further diminished by gasworks and breweries. The scrolled ironwork of the railings on either side of the Palace are part of the same campaign. This drastic action left the surroundings of the Palace so bald-looking that there were various schemes to ameliorate the effect. In 1920 the Forecourt became the site for the Scottish National Memorial to the late King, Edward VII. His statue by

H.S. Gamley faces the Tower and the Abbey and is set off by a curved screen wall designed by the architect G. Washington Browne. His scheme embraces the entrance gateways to the north and south with their gatepiers topped by lions and unicorns supporting the ornamented wrought-iron gates and screens carried out under the supervision of J. Starkie Gardner. The gates bear images of St Andrew and the Holyrood stag with prominent thistles. The ghost of the Gothic arcade on the north flank is all that survives from James IV's great gatehouse which was destroyed in 1753.

THE PIAZZAS lead directly into the Great Stair. If the exterior façades of Bruce's courtyard are distinguished by their chaste classicism, the interior is baroque. In the Scottish Palace of the restored Stuart dynasty architecture was used to impress and to awe.

The partially cantilevered broad stone flights of the Great Stair were at the limit of building technology. The massive stone balusters add to the grandeur of this first stage on the processional route to the King's Apartments. High above is the first of the spectacular ceilings by the English plasterers, Houlbert and Dunsterfield. The central compartment is surrounded by tiers of hand-modelled flowers and swags built up on wires to give a luxuriant three-dimensional effect. The life-sized figures of angels in the corners burst from their frames to brandish the symbols of kingship. Sadly the central circular compartment never received its illusionistic decorative painting. Of the three doorcases at the top of the stair, remodelled *c.* 1800, that on the right leads to Charles II's Council Chamber in Bruce's replica of James V's Tower, which has another spectacular fretwork ceiling; that straight ahead to the King's Bedroom down an impressive enfilade of doorways; that on the left to the Queen's Guard-room. The glass lantern was supplied by a grace-and-favour tenant.

RIGHT: *Detail of a Brussels tapestry:* The Bacchanalian Feast *from the Planets series*

AS THE outermost room of the Queen's suite, the Guardroom would have been plainly finished in keeping with its function. Thus no earlier decorative scheme prevented it from being transformed *c.* 1800 by its grace-and-favour tenant into an elegant neoclassical reception room in the Adam style. Sadly the scheme is undocumented. The plasterer was perhaps inspired by a spirit of rivalry with the virtuoso quality of the surrounding Carolean plasterwork to produce work of equal refinement, where the plaster flowers float on the friezes. The Ionic screen helps disguise the awkward blank behind the royal arms in the centre of the west front. It is not known if this room always had windows on both sides. Only those to the west have handsome matching surrounds.

This room was first used as the Royal Dining Room at the end of Queen Victoria's reign. Previously it had been part of the Duke of Hamilton's suite. Thomas Hall, the Edinburgh decorators, claim credit for decorating it in their advertising brochure of *c.* 1900, but there may have been further changes in 1910 when the grate was installed for King George V.

Sir David Wilkie: George IV

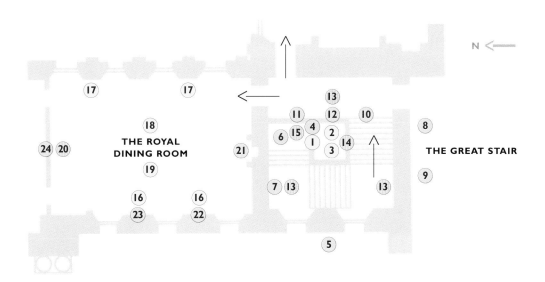

THE GREAT STAIR

FURNITURE

1 Pair of giltwood pier tables by Whytock and Reid, made for two 18th-century alabaster tops formerly in the collection of Pope Pius VI. Presented to King George V in 1917.

2 Set of carved oak side chairs, late 17th-century style.

3 Sedan chair reputed to have belonged to the Scottish ballad-writer Carolina, Baroness Nairne (1766-1845), late 18th-century.

PICTURES

4 Stanley Cursiter: *The Queen Receiving the Honours of Scotland, St Giles Cathedral, Edinburgh, 24 June 1953*, 1954.

5 David Donaldson: *Queen Elizabeth II*, 1967

6 Lattanzio Gambara: *Diana*

7 Lattanzio Gambara: *Mercury*

8-10 Lattanzio Gambara: *Three scenes from the Wedding of Pirithöus and Hippodamia*

11 Lattanzio Gambara: *An Allegory (Fortitude and Charity)*

12 Lattanzio Gambara: *Neptune and Caenis*

Fresco fragments transferred to canvas from the Palazzo Pedrocca, Scaglia, Brescia, c. 1550.

TAPESTRIES

13 Four Brussels panels from The Planets series, late 16th century. Moved from Hampton Court Palace to Holyroodhouse c. 1860.

(north, upper)	The Triumph of Mars
(north, lower)	The Toilet of Venus
(south)	Bacchanalian Feast
(east)	Mars and Venus

ARMS

14 Two cases each containing a trophy of three arrows. Presented by the Royal Company of Archers to King Edward VII, 1903, and to King George V, 1911.

15 Two trophies of basket-hilted broadswords, 18th-19th centuries.

THE ROYAL DINING ROOM

FURNITURE

16 Pair of giltwood pier tables with marble tops, mid-18th-century. style.

17 Pair of mahogany pier tables by Young, Trotter and Hamilton of Edinburgh. Part of a large group of furniture made for the apartments of the Comte d'Artois in 1796 during his exile at Holyroodhouse.

18 Set of mahogany rail-back dining chairs, late 18th century.

19 Mahogany five-pedestal dining table, early 19th century.

PORCELAIN

20 Derby white and gold part dessert service, early 19th century.

PICTURES

21 John Michael Wright: *Lord Mungo Murray, c. 1683* (on loan from the 1st Lord Forteviot Trust).

22 Louis-Gabriel Blanchet: *Prince Henry Benedict Stuart, c. 1739*.

23 Louis-Gabriel Blanchet: *Prince Charles Edward Stuart*, 1739.

24 Sir David Wilkie: *George IV*, 1829.

THIS ROOM has been altered more often than any other room in the Palace. The changes can be followed in the many engravings and photographs of the interiors of Holyroodhouse. As Charles II's Guardroom it was simply finished with a plain cornice. In 1822 it became the most important room in the Palace when it was fitted up as the Great Drawing Room on the occasion of George IV's state visit to Scotland. This dramatic change of use probably arose because nobody could remember the original room sequence. George IV was given exclusive use of the Great Stair, while his subjects entered from the east, to the reverse of Charles II's careful planning. The new Throne Room was hung with crimson cloth with matching 'gorgeous' continued curtain draperies by Trotter's. The throne and canopy made for Queen Charlotte, mother of George IV, was sent north from Buckingham House to lend a splash of metropolitan glamour to dowdy Holyroodhouse.

Sir George Hayter, Queen Victoria

The ancient crown of the kings of Scotland was presented to George IV while he sat on the throne.

In 1842 the room was rehung with 'crimson merino damask' for Queen Victoria's state visit. After 1850, when the Queen had taken up residence in the royal apartments and the Carolean oak panelling had been stripped of its later white paint, the Throne Room must have appeared tawdry. Although money was always tight, enough was found to install a new plaster ceiling bearing the royal arms in 1856. Robert Matheson designed this to 'accord' with the 'continuous suite'. A new cornice with intertwined thistles, roses, lilies and shamrocks was modelled by the plasterers John Ramage & Son. Because of pressure on space this important room had to double-up as the Dining Room until the present Royal Dining Room was released by the dislodging of persistent grace-and-favour tenants at the end of her reign.

Matheson's oak-grained ceiling was described as 'dreadful' by Queen Mary. Although it was claimed that the 'dignity of Scotland' was at stake, it had to be painted out economically until money was found to refit the entire room in 1929 to the designs of J. Wilson Paterson of the Office of Works, who wrote: 'The draped canopied Throne, the ribbed ceiling and other early Victorian work was swept away, and finishings appropriate to the Palace and in harmony

Paul van Somer, James I

with the work of Sir William Bruce were substituted. The design of the richly modelled plaster ceiling is based on the lines of other original ones, but care has been taken that it is not in any sense a mere copy, and a more modern treatment has been adopted.'

Paterson's new oak panelling, in the Doric order, had to incorporate a number of full-length Royal portraits and was made by Scott Morton and Co, the Edinburgh architectural woodworkers. They also supplied a pair of new thrones in 1931 for the recess which was 'cut in the thick wall'. To modern taste the effect is lifeless, especially the repetitive fibrous plaster with its monograms of King George V and Queen Mary under the imperial crown. The discarded throne canopy was presented to the National Museums, but Queen Charlotte's magnificent throne has never been seen again.

THE NEXT five rooms of the King's Apartments retain most of their Carolean decoration, which builds up to a climax in the King's Bedroom. The Evening Drawing Room was Charles II's Presence Chamber. Houlbert and Dunsterfield's fretwork ceiling has vigorous scrolls and panels of interwoven laurel branches at its end, but the effect is weakened without the intended painting in the central quatrefoil panel. The bolection-moulded red marble chimney-piece is the first of a series in a varied selection of marbles, contributing to the baroque opulence. Bruce liked a correct architectural effect in his interiors and must have chosen the frieze with oak leaves to suit the Ionic order he had selected for this room.

This room was modernized with wallpaper in the late eighteenth century. After Queen Victoria's return, the four panels of Brussels tapestry were sent from Buckingham Palace in 1851 to give an air of richness and warmth. The largest panels on the end walls depict the continents of Africa and Asia. The Court used this room as a general sitting room.

King George V replaced the wallpaper with oak. In their zeal to create a neo-Carolean character, the architects of the Office of Works mistakenly disposed of the pair of Ionic pilasters framing the chimney-piece. King George V refitted the Victorian plate-glass windows with their original small panes.

TOP: *After Teniers:* The Fish Market, c. *1750*

ABOVE: *French gilt settee and chairs by E. Saint-Georges, covered with Beauvais tapestry*

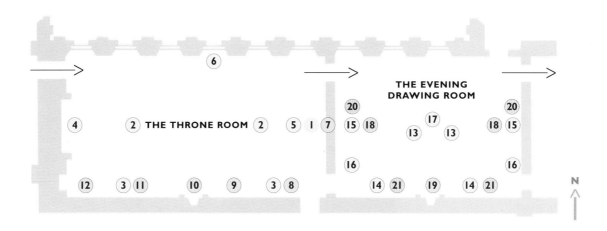

THE THRONE ROOM

FURNITURE

1 French gilt bronze and alabaster mantel clock by Brysons, Paris, late 19th-century.

2 Pair of gilt metal chandeliers copied from the 18th-century silver original by Francis Garthorne at Hampton Court Palace.

3 Set of six giltwood x-frame stools, 19th-century. Of the same design as an 18th-century set at Hampton Court Palace.

4 Pair of upholstered throne chairs made for King George V and Queen Mary by Morris & Co. of London, 1911.

5 Giltwood side table of 18th-century design.

6 Part of a set of oak window stools with needlework covers made to celebrate the Coronation of King George VI and Queen Elizabeth, 1937.

PICTURES

7 Paul van Somer: *James VI & I*, 1618.

8 Sir Peter Lely: *Charles II*, c. 1665-70.

9 Sir Peter Lely: *Catherine of Braganza*, c. 1663-5.

10 Sir George Hayter: *Queen Victoria*, 1838.

11 Sir Peter Lely: *James VII & II when Duke of York*, c. 1665.

12 Sir Peter Lely: *Mary of Modena when Duchess of York*, c. 1675-80.

Sir Peter Lely, Charles II

THE EVENING DRAWING ROOM

FURNITURE

13 Set of six French giltwood armchairs and a sofa by Etienne Saint-Georges, upholstered in Beauvais tapestry woven with La Fontaine's fables, c. 1745.

14 Pair of ebonized pier tables with marble tops, early 19th century.

15 Pair of gilt gesso side tables, early 18th-century.

16 Set of mahogany and parcel-gilt side chairs, mid-18th century.

17 Silver-plated chandelier copied from the 18th-century silver original by Francis Garthorne at Hampton Court Palace.

PORCELAIN

18 Two Chinese export porcelain punch bowls, 18th century.

PICTURES

19 Sir William Hutchinson: *Queen Elizabeth The Queen Mother*, 1967.

TAPESTRIES

20 Two Brussels panels from the Four Continents, workshop of Peter and Franz van der Borght, c. 1750. Formerly at Buckingham Palace.

(east)   Asia
(west)   Africa

21 Two Brussels 'Teniers' panels, workshop of Franz van der Borght, c. 1750. Formerly at Buckingham Palace.

(south, left)   The Vegetable Market
(south, right)   The Fish Market

Detail of an early 18th-century pier table

THE INCREASING richness of the decorations in this room, which was Charles II's Privy Chamber, indicates the ever more exclusive character of each successive interior on the progression through his suite. To underline this impression Bruce selected the Corinthian order for the pilasters which frame the dark green marble chimney-piece and support an appropriately enriched Corinthian entablature which breaks forward over the pilasters and then continues as the cornice around the room. The pedestals which support these pilasters are continued round the room as the dado.

Of the many who tried to emulate it, only the Duke of Lauderdale at Thirlestane Castle managed to achieve anything like the richness of Houlbert and Dunsterfield's astounding illusionistic plasterwork in this room, where the swags surrounding the central compartment plunge down into the room and are apparently restrained by ribbons. In the corners the King's wreathed cipher is borne aloft by eagles and cherubs. Heraldic unicorns spring from delicately modelled rose-heads in the long central panels. The chimney-piece is enriched with equally lively fleshy carving by the Dutch sculptor, Jan van Santvoort, to frame a decorative painting of Cupid and Psyche, by the Dutch artist, Jacob de Wet. The French tapestries, illustrating the history of Diana, were probably

One of a pair of 18th-century giltwood pier tables

purchased for Charles II in 1668 from the Edinburgh merchant, John Coupar, for £90 and have hung in this room at least since 1796.

They were well suited to the antiquarian mood cultivated in the renovations for Queen Victoria in 1850. This east-facing room was her Private Drawing Room. The Edinburgh decorator D. R. Hay painted the ceiling in rich colours to complement the tapestries. After the intervention of the Duke of Hamilton 'with his superior taste and great experience in his own magnificent Palace', enough money was released to gild the ceiling. De Wet's painting was deemed unsuitable, however, and was replaced with looking glass. The ceiling was deemed to be in doubtful taste after George V's state visit in 1911 and was painted out in white during the general de-Victorianization.

THE KING'S
ANTE-CHAMBER

Although this room is richly decorated with its pink and white marble chimney-piece, the plasterwork is more restrained to suit the smaller scale and function of this room. De Wet's overmantel painting depicts Acis and Galatea, but the central panel of the ceiling lacks its decorative painting and thus attention rests on the grotesque clawed monsters which form auricular cartouches in its corners and the illusionistic plaster ribbons threaded through its mouldings.

The door in the west wall leads through to the Page of the Back Stairs' Room. The page's role was to control access to the back stairs which played such an important role in court life. This room was Queen Victoria's bedroom in 1850.

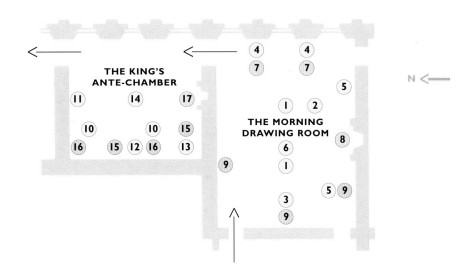

THE MORNING DRAWING ROOM

FURNITURE

1   Pair of mahogany sofas and set of side chairs, mid-18th century, the chairs with needlework made in the 1920s by a group of Ladies of Scotland for Queen Mary.

2   Mahogany tripod polescreen with contemporary needlework, mid-18th century.

3   Walnut writing table, late 17th century. Similar to a table made for William III at Hampton Court Palace.

4   Pair of giltwood pier tables and glasses, the tables with the arms and heraldic supporters of the Duchess of Gordon, mother of Lord Adam Gordon, c. 1770. Recorded at Holyroodhouse since 1782.

5   Pair of walnut tables with grey marble tops, mid-18th century.

6   Silver-plated chandelier copied from the 18th-century silver original by Francis Garthorne at Hampton Court Palace.

PORCELAIN

7   Pair of Chinese blue and white bowls, 18th century.

PICTURES

8   Jacob de Wet the Younger: *Landscape with a River with Figures, c. 1675.*

TAPESTRIES

9   Four French (Paris) panels panels from the History of Diana, c. 1630. Probably purchased for Charles II in 1668.

(south, right)   Niobe protests at the worship of Latona

(west)   Diana petitioning Jupiter

(north)   Actaeon turned into a stag and The birth of Diana and Apollo (flanking a Flemish panel of Tobit and Anna, early 17th century)

THE KING'S ANTE-CHAMBER

FURNITURE

10   Ten ebonized side chairs upholstered in modern red velvet, late 17th century. Formerly in the Poulet collection, Hinton House, Somerset.

11   German marquetry cabinet, late 16th-century, on later English walnut stand.

12   Oyster-veneered walnut cabinet on stand, late 17th-century.

13   Walnut longcase clock by J. Windmills, London, early 18th-century.

14   Cut-glass eight-branch chandelier, mid-18th century.

TAPESTRIES

15   Two Flemish panels from the Aeneid, late 16th-century. Recorded at Holyroodhouse since 1685.

(south, right)   The Death of Dido

(west, above door)   The meeting of Dido and Aeneas

16   Two French (Paris) panels from the History of Diana, c. 1630. *En suite* with four in Morning Drawing Room.

(west, left)   The death of Orion

(west, right)   The destruction of the Children of Niobe

PICTURES

17   Jacob de Wet the Younger: *The Triumph of Galatea, c. 1675.*

THE SUPREMACY of this room is made clear in the elaboration of its decoration, in which the finest plasterwork, decorative painting and carving in the Palace are blended with the tapestries into a baroque unity, and through its position on the central axis, like Louis XIV's Bedroom (from 1701) at Versailles. This axial thrust would have continued out into the Privy Garden (its walls have now gone) to the east, which this room overlooked.

This is the only ceiling to be completed with illusionistic decorative painting. It depicts *The Apotheosis of Hercules*, intended as a compliment to the King by comparing him with the legendary hero. De Wet strove to give the viewer the impression of looking up into a sky peopled with gods; the animals, including owls, sheep and spaniels, peering down from the brink add to the illusion. The corners are counter-changed rather than identical and the crowned thistle of Scotland makes its first appearance. De Wet followed his flattering comparison through into his overmantel painting where this toughest of infants is seen dispatching snakes. The baroque luxuriance of materials is built up by Hercules' golden cradle. The silver chair of the nursemaid recalls the silver furniture of Versailles. The sculpted surround of the overmantel and the lions framing the marble chimney-piece are as deeply undercut as the plasterwork, and the draperies as

ABOVE: *Ceiling painting:* Hercules Admitted to Olympia

richly embroidered as the King's bed would have been.

The panelling is no less ornamented and the formality of the room is underlined by the strong vertical emphasis created by the continued over-doors. This dark oak panelling has never been bleached, as it has in the preceding rooms, but its depth of colour may be due to Trotter's workmen, who stripped it of its later eighteenth-century white paint in 1850 and high-varnished it.

The door in the west wall leads to the King's Dressing Room. From 1850 until his death, the Prince Consort used the Bed Chamber as his dressing room. A contemporary watercolour shows his portable shower-bath.

In 1976, it was decided to display this room as a baroque bedroom using the late seventeenth-century state bed from the Duke of Hamilton's apartments.

THE LOBBY

This little lobby led to the King's Stool Room which contained his close-stool, but its decoration is no less rich or carefully considered. The borrowed light, which appears to be original, lights a mezzanine which may have been for the King's valet.

In 1850, D. R. Hay painted the miniature dome with its vases of flowers in the spandrels 'deep azure' and sprinkled it with silver stars. In 1850 the Prince Consort's valet occupied the mezzanine.

THE KING'S CLOSET

The private character of this small room is made clear by the intimate effect created by the coved ceiling. The spandrels of the ceiling are decorated appropriately for a King's private study with military trophies; and this theme continues through into the antique armour framing the overmantel which projects boldly into the room. In the cove, with its shell corners, the royal arms of Scotland are paired with fantastic cartouches on which the King's cipher is supported by lions. De Wet's overmantel painting shows *The Finding of Moses*, alluding to the mythical descent of the Scottish kings from Pharaoh's daughter, Scota.

In 1850 this room became Queen Victoria's Breakfast Room and was hung with a green and gold flock-paper.

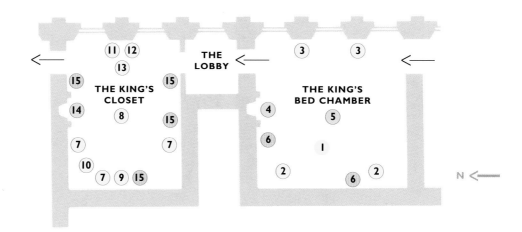

THE KING'S BED CHAMBER

FURNITURE

1 State bed with crimson damask upholstery, largely renewed, c. 1680. Originally in the Duke of Hamilton's apartments and in the 19th century exhibited as Mary Queen of Scots' bed.

2 Four lacquered and ebonized armchairs and one side chair with modern upholstery, late 17th century.

3 Two walnut pier tables, two walnut mirrors and two pairs of walnut candle stands, late 17th century.

PICTURES

4 Jacob de Wet the Younger: *The Infant Hercules strangling the Serpents*, c. 1675.

5 Jacob de Wet the Younger: *Hercules admitted to Olympus*, 1675.

TAPESTRIES

6 Two Brussels panels from the History of Alexander; workshop of Jan Leyniers, mid-17th century. Recorded at Holyroodhouse from before 1700.

(west)   Alexander wounded in the thigh

(north)   The Lion Hunt

THE KING'S CLOSET

FURNITURE

7 Five lacquered and ebonized chairs with modern green damask upholstery, late 17th century.

8 Lacquered two-manual harpsichord with false inscription of Johannes Rucker of Antwerp and date 1636, French, mid-18th century.

9 Chinese lacquer cabinet, 18th century, on later ebonized stand.

10 Black lacquered and gilt harp by Holtzman, Paris, early 19th century.

11 Pair of giltwood candle stands, late 17th century.

12 Ebonized and silvered pier table with mermaid legs, late 17th century.

13 Carved limewood pier glass, late 17th century.

PICTURES

14 Jacob de Wet the Younger: *The Finding of Moses*, c. 1675.

TAPESTRIES

15 Four English (Mortlake) panels from the Life of Diogenes, late 17th century. Purchased for Charles II in 1683.

(west)   The meeting of Alexander and Diogenes

(south)   Diogenes meditating

(south)   Diogenes visited by Plato

(north)   Diogenes beside his barrel

THE GREAT GALLERY connects the King's New Apartment to the east with the Queen's rooms in the old Royal Apartment to the west in James V's Tower. Irregularities in its form suggest that it incorporates earlier walls. The close proximity of the Abbey is apparent in the cluster of buttresses obscuring the east windows. Bruce devised a classical scheme with Doric surrounds to the pair of black marble chimney-pieces. They are framed by Ionic pilasters supporting a cornice enriched with scrollwork and figures.

The special decorative character of the Gallery was established in February 1684 when de Wet was contracted to supply portraits of the 110 real and legendary kings of Scotland from Fergus I to Charles II. De Wet certainly drew on the similar series painted by George Jamieson for one of the triumphal arches erected in honour of Charles I's Coronation in Edinburgh in 1633.

The artist has been idly criticized for making the ancient kings look the same, but this was a serious attempt to preserve the likenesses of the more recent Stuarts. The long line of paintings reasserted the Stuarts' divine right to rule in the face of the recent regicide and anticipated the nineteenth-century concept of the Scottish National Portrait Gallery. The contract attached as much importance to the inscriptions bearing the king's 'name, age, the years of reign and date of the world'

as to any concept of likeness as the series stretched back in time.

The series seems to have been conceived as freely hanging paintings: there was no attempt to relate them to the panels over the chimney-pieces or the overdoors. Charles II is depicted standing next to a table with fantastic gilded eagle legs, which might reflect something of the character of the furnishings of his new Scottish Palace, had it ever been completed.

The paintings are said to have been 'slashed by the sabres' of English troops quartered in the palace after the 1745 rebellion; archaeological evidence found during conservation has confirmed this. Especial violence was reserved for the portrait of Mary Queen of Scots. By 1826 they had been 'repaired and, after having been

removed from their hanging frames, fixed in the panels of the wainscoting'; but a number still hung loose in the window-embrasures at the end of the nineteenth century.

This room, the largest in the Palace, has served many purposes. It was used for the election of Scotland's representative peers after the Union of the Parliaments in 1707. George V made it into the State Dining Room, improving the service arrangements in the rooms to the north; tapestry-covered screens were 'placed at the ends of the table to shorten the room'. When the floors of the rooms above were strengthened in 1968, the opportunity was taken to install a new ornamental ceiling to take away the 'tunnel-like' appearance of the room: designed by George Hay, it was executed by Albert Cram.

MARY QUEEN OF SCOTS' bedroom is the most famous room in Scotland and, during the nineteenth century, the apartments associated with Mary Queen of Scots were described as 'perhaps the most interesting suite of rooms in Europe'. This long tradition of expectation makes it difficult to disentangle fact from fantasy.

These rooms were almost certainly the Queen's Rooms in the Upper Apartment of James V's Tower. In Bruce's remodelling of the Palace they lost their importance when new apartments for the King and Queen were relocated on the first floor. It was probably because of this demotion that the original sixteenth-century oak-panelled ceilings on this floor were not replaced by fashionable plasterwork rather than through any feelings of sentiment. Sash windows were inserted and the woodwork partially renewed. The chimney-piece was given a Doric surround and an Ionic overmantel characteristic of Bruce, but there was no attempt to upgrade the stone fireplace surround with fashionable marble jambs as in the rooms below.

When, in the late eighteenth century, the attention of visitors began to focus on this portion of the Palace, showing the rooms to visitors became a profitable perquisite of the servants of the Duke of Hamilton, who had taken possession of this part of the Palace. Because the servants were tipped for their services, they were naturally anxious to be

François Clouet: Mary Queen of Scots

The Darnley jewel, c. 1570

Lithograph of Mary Queen of Scots' Bedroom by Swarbreck, 1838

the next apartment, the rage of his enemies put an end to his life, piercing his body with fifty-six wounds.

The room's popular success owed a great deal to the visual seductiveness of its advanced state of decay, especially of the textiles – which the Duke's housekeeper was careful to promote – giving an air of far greater antiquity than the reality, and its melancholy and faded aspect was in admirable keeping with its tale of sorrow and crime.

When in 1855 responsibility for showing the rooms passed to the Office of Works, a new professionalism was applied to an amateur creation. By this time the story was as ineradicable as the famous bloodstains and both George IV and Queen Victoria had commanded that the rooms should be regarded as sacrosanct. It was impossible, though, to obey the royal injunction, as the pressure of visitors required repairs to be made to the floorboards and, for their own preservation, the tattered hangings of the 'Supping Room' had to be preserved under glass. Thus by a series of small steps the seductive air of decay began to be eroded in the face of a new spruceness. At the same time the development of furniture history meant that sophisticated visitors began to realize that that the furniture could not possibly be earlier than the late seventeenth century. It is perhaps surprising, given the anxiety to clutch at

seen to be giving value for money: thus they became adept at telling the chilling details of the story of the brutal murder of Rizzio said to have taken place here. Their storyline was improved and tested against visitors' reactions through the years. By degrees, the Dukes made improvements to their rooms and relegated their old-fashioned and shabby baroque furniture to the floor above where they were recycled and inextricably woven into the tale of Mary Queen of Scots. Thus the Duke's old red damask state bed became transformed into 'the couch of the Rose of Scotland'; and the servants rescued other 'relics', such as the Queen's workbox, and installed various reputed illustrations of the principal figures in the stories of both the murder and the Queen's own martyrdom. An early nineteenth-century guidebook describes how

Strangers visiting the palace are usually led to Queen Mary's apartments, in the second floor of which her own bed still remains. It is of crimson damask, bordered with green silk fringes and tassels, but is now almost in tatters ... Close to the floor of this room, a piece of wainscot, about three feet square, hangs upon hinges, and opens a passage to a trap-stair, which communicates with the apartments below. Through this passage Darnley and his accomplices rushed in to murder the unhappy Rizzio, on the 9th of March 1566. The Queen, when this outrage took place, was at supper, in a closet adjoining her bedchamber, with the Countess of Argyle, Rizzio, and a few domestics. Rizzio, on perceiving the conspirators enter, headed by Lord Ruthven in complete armour, instantly supposed he was the victim, and took refuge behind the Queen. But, in spite of her tears and entreaties, he was torn from her presence, and, before he could be dragged through

Hans Eworth (attributed to): Henry Stewart, Lord Darnley and his brother, Charles Stewart, 5th Earl of Lennox

anything that was genuine amid so much that was apparently bogus, that although the Jacobean painted frieze was discovered earlier this century, it was as late as 1976 that the room was finally dismantled to display the frieze in its entirety. It was then felt that the baroque furniture could be more sympathetically displayed in the contemporary King's Apartment.

The *trompe-l'oeil* painted 'plaster' frieze was probably added to the room in 1617 in preparation for James VI's visit to Scotland. It would have given a superficial air of modernity to his grandfather's Tower. The royal arms of the ceiling were probably also updated at the same time. Since 'Queen Mary's furniture' has not stood the test of scholarly scrutiny, it is perhaps a surprise to learn that these rooms do appear to fit contemporary accounts of Rizzio's murder.

The three rooms which comprise the Mary Queen of Scots' Chambers have recently been rearranged in the spirit of the Swarbreck lithograph (page 23). Included in the display are a number of Stuart relics and momentos formerly housed in Windsor Castle.

TOP: *Anon., Flemish school, sixteenth century:* The Family of Henry VII with St George and the Dragon
ABOVE: *Livinus de Vogelaare:* The Memorial of Lord Darnley

SUPPER
ROOM

MARY QUEEN
OF SCOTS'
BED
CHAMBER

MARY QUEEN
OF SCOTS'
OUTER
CHAMBER

The major works of art and relics in Mary Queen of Scots' Chambers are listed below.

Mary Queen of Scots' pomander

MARY QUEEN OF SCOTS' OUTER CHAMBER

TAPESTRIES

Five Flemish verdure or forest panels, late 17th century.

PICTURES

Livinius de Vogelaare: *The Memorial of Lord Darnley*, 1567-8.

Anon., Flemish School, sixteenth century: *The Family of Henry VII with St George and the Dragon*, c. 1505-9.

Anon., British School, sixteenth century: *James VI and I*, c. 1587.

Attributed to Hans Eworth: *Henry, Lord Darnley and his brother Charles, 5th Earl of Lennox*, 1562.

François Clouet: *Mary Queen of Scots*, 1558 (miniature).

THE STUART RELICS

The royal collection of Stuart relics was largely formed by Queen Mary (consort of King George V) in the early years of this century. Among the authentic pieces there are a number of objects with only a traditional or a commemorative association with the Stuart dynasty.

MARY QUEEN OF SCOTS' RELICS

The Darnley Jewel. Gold enamel and jewelled locket made for Margaret Douglas, Countess of Lennox, mother of Lord Darnley c. 1570. Purchased by Queen Victoria in 1842.

Three needlework panels, c. 1575. The work of Mary Queen of Scots. Formerly at Oxburgh Hall, Norfolk.

Silver pomander, late 16th century. Reputed to have belonged to Mary Queen of Scots.

Rosary and crucifix, possibly late 16th century. Reputed to have belonged to Mary Queen of Scots.

Locket containing hair of Mary Queen of Scots. Bequeathed to Queen Victoria by Lord Belhaven in 1862.

Ebony scarlet tortoiseshell and silver-mounted cabinet on later ebonized stand, probably Flemish, late 17th century. Formerly held to have belonged to Mary Queen of Scots and bequeathed to Queen Victoria by Lord Belhaven in 1862.

Embroidered box, 17th century. Formerly held to have belonged to Mary Queen of Scots.

RELICS OF JAMES VI AND I, CHARLES I AND CHARLES II

Needlework layette or baby-clothes basket. Reputed to have been used for James VI and I.

Lace baby clothes and box, 17th century. Reputed to have belonged to Charles I. Purchased by The Queen in 1959.

South German ebony dressing case with silver mounts, early 17th century, containing brush, scissors, comb etc. Traditionally held to have belonged to Charles I. Purchased by King George V.

The Little Gidding Casket, 17th century. Containing pieces of embroidery etc. Said to have belonged to Charles I. Purchased by Queen Victoria from a descendant of the family of Nicholas Ferrar.

Jane Lane's watch, 17th century. Given by King Charles II to Jane Lane in 1651 after the Battle of Worcester and presented to King George V by a descendant in 1928.

Detail from the Oxburgh Panels

Ceiling detail from Mary Queen of Scots' Outer Chamber

RELICS OF LATER STUARTS

Silver gilt caddinet by L. Valadier, Rome, c. 1790. Made for Henry Benedict, Cardinal York, brother of the Young Pretender. Acquired by Queen Mary in 1919.

Maiolica dish and gilt spoon. Bequeathed to George III by Cardinal York in 1807.

Agate-handled knife and fork, 18th century. Belonged to the Young Pretender. Captured at Culloden in 1745 and given to King George IV in 1820.

Pair of miniature pistols, 18th century. Reputed to have belonged to the Young Pretender.

Basket-hilt sword, 18th century. Reputed to have belonged to the Young Pretender. Given to King George V in 1926.

MARY QUEEN OF SCOTS' BED CHAMBER

TAPESTRIES

Four Flemish (Antwerp) panels of the History of Phaeton, mid to late 17th-century.

The Little Gidding Casket, 17th century

(clockwise) Apollo and Phaeton, Clymene and Phaeton, The Sisters of Phaeton, The Fall of Phaeton

PICTURES

Andrea Schiavone: *The Adoration of the Kings, c.* 1560.

FURNITURE

South German pictorial marquetry cabinet, late 16th-century and later.

Oak draw-leaf table in 16th-century style, 19th century.

Bed hangings of crewel-work, late 17th century, on modern frame.

THE SUPPER ROOM

TAPESTRIES

Flemish verdure or forest panels, late 17th century.

Silver gilt caddinet by L. Valadier

Sixteenth-century timber ceiling of Mary Queen of Scots' Bed Chamber enriched in 1617

THIS IS, confusingly, the original King's Bedroom of James V's Tower. In 1528 the two additional inner rooms provided in the round corner-towers must have seemed the height of planning sophistication, but by the standards of a queen in 1671 the accommodation was inadequate. Additional service rooms were therefore provided in a wing which joined the Tower to the north. Even Bruce was unable to impose much regularity on the Queen's Bed Chamber but he built up the sense of increasing grandeur by framing the chimney-piece with Corinthian pilasters to indicate its importance. In 1740 the Duke of Hamilton carried out extensive renovations following his marriage to his third wife in 1738. The Duchess was given a fashionable new bedroom designed by the architect William Adam in the adjacent wing and the rooms were refurnished in the latest style. Unfortunately the wing was demolished during George IV's improvements after 1822; the characteristic dove-coloured chimney-piece supplied by William Adam's marble works is the sole survivor of this elegance.

The bed now shown was moved here in the early twentieth century when Queen Mary's Outer Chamber on the floor above was 'renovated'. For almost a century it had been passed off as Charles I's bed. It was actually supplied by John Ridge, a London upholsterer, to the Duke of Hamilton in 1682. The Duke paid £218. 10s. 0d. for 'a crimson and gould velvet bed, lined with satin with 8 chairs and velvet cases, a feather bed and bolster, quilts Japanned glass and stands a footstool, blankets'. The quality of its fringes, which incorporated silk-covered wire flowers in baskets, only became apparent after recent conservation. During William Adam's series of improvements in 1740, this bed was given mahogany footposts. In 1745 the Young Pretender occupied the Duke of Hamilton's Apartments at Holyroodhouse and slept in it, and he was followed shortly afterwards by the Duke of Cumberland.

William Wissing: Posthumous portrait of James, Duke of Cambridge

THIS ROOM and the previous room comprise the original King's Apartment in James V's Tower of 1528–32. The great thickness of the walls betray its defensive quality. These rooms were refitted by Bruce after 1671 but they retain a Scottish vernacular character. The new black marble chimney-piece is framed by a pair of Ionic pilasters, but although the new ceiling looks like those in the King's rooms, it is of old-fashioned cast, rather than hand-modelled, plaster. The doors have typical Scottish panels and the character of the room reveals that the efforts of the skilled Dutch and English craftsmen were concentrated in the King's rooms with their more fashionable detailing.

During the eighteenth century this room became the Duke of Hamilton's Dining Room and had handsome early Georgian furniture with cabriole legs. In 1855 the Office of Works assumed responsibility for showing these rooms to the public (they were added on to the tour of Mary Queen of Scots' rooms) and in 1864 acquired the set of Mortlake tapestries depicting playing boys to replace the Duke's paper-hangings. The tapestries were part of a remarkable collection of furniture assembled by R. G. Ellis, an Edinburgh lawyer, during the previous '20 or 30 years of labour'. The collection, rather surprisingly, had only three provenances: the Royal Palaces of Holyroodhouse, Falkland and Dunfermline, while a

chair reputedly came from 'Glasgow Cathedral'. Whatever the truth of these origins, the collection now has considerable antiquarian interest in

its own right. It was displayed in the three first-floor rooms (the old Royal Apartment) which became known as the 'Darnley Rooms'.

ABOVE AND RIGHT: *Mortlake tapestry, the Playing Boys series*

THE LOBBY was also part of the old Royal Apartment, refitted in 1671 to serve as the Queen's Apartment. Although the room was old and irregular, Bruce was no less anxious to impose an architectural order: here the new marble chimney-piece was framed by a pair of Ionic pilasters and the vertical emphasis was followed through in the continued overmantel and overdoors to create a formal effect. The character of these rooms remains simple in comparison with the baroque splendours of the King's Apartment where the efforts of the most skilful craftsmen were concentrated.

Because no queen ever came, her Apartment was appropriated by the Duke and Duchess of Hamilton, the Hereditary Keepers of the Palace, who introduced sumptuous baroque furniture. From time to time their successors modernized these rooms by introducing paperhangings and new furniture.

When in 1855, after Queen Victoria's return to the Palace, responsibility for showing 'the Historical Apartments' – previously profitably undertaken by the Duke's servants – was assumed by the Office of Works, the Duke was compensated with apartments above the Great Gallery. His old rooms were redecorated in an antiquarian mode to harmonize with those of Mary Queen of Scots and old furniture and tapestry were collected to replace the modern paperhangings.

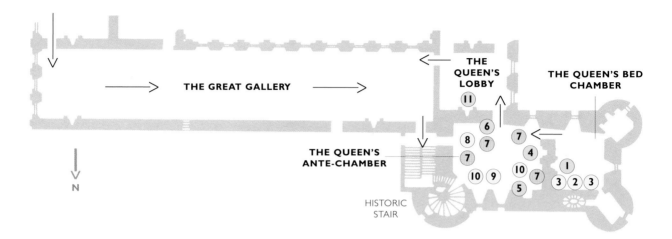

THE GREAT GALLERY →

THE QUEEN'S LOBBY ← 11

THE QUEEN'S BED CHAMBER ←

6
8 7   7
7   4
10 9   10 7   1
5   3 2 3

THE QUEEN'S ANTE-CHAMBER

HISTORIC STAIR

N

THE GREAT GALLERY

FURNITURE

Group of oak, walnut and beech caned chairs, late 17th century.

Tam O'Shanter's chair, carved oak with brass panels, early 19th century. Acquired by King George IV in 1822 and sent to Holyroodhouse by King Edward VII in 1901.

PICTURES

Jacob de Wet the Younger: individual portraits of the rulers of Scotland from Fergus I to Charles II, 1684.

HISTORIC STAIR

PICTURES

William Aikman: *John Campbell, 2nd Duke of Argyll and Duke of Greenwich*, c. 1709.

THE QUEEN'S BED CHAMBER

PICTURES

1 William Wissing: *Posthumous portrait of James, Duke of Cambridge*, c. 1685 (overmantel).

FURNITURE

2 Tester bed upholstered in crimson and gold velvet and yellow satin (part renewed). Supplied in 1682 to the Duke of Hamilton by the London upholsterer John Ridge for £218 10s.

3 Two ebonized wing chairs, modern upholstery, late 17th century.

THE QUEEN'S ANTE-CHAMBER

PICTURES

4 Sir Peter Lely: *Princess Isabella*, 1677 (overmantel).

5 Anon., North Italian School, sixteenth century: *James 'the Admirable' Crichton*, c. 1580.

6 Francesco Fieravino: *Still-life of Fruit and Flowers with a Carpet*, c. 1650.

TAPESTRIES

7 Four English (Mortlake) panels from The Playing Boys series, first half of the 17th century. Purchased from the Edinburgh antiquarian R.G. Ellis in 1864.

FURNITURE

8 Dutch marquetry centre table, 19th century.

9 Electrotype copy of a silver pier glass and table at Windsor Castle made for Charles II.

10 Part of a group of walnut or beech side chairs with original Turkey-work upholstery, late 17th century. Bought for Holyroodhouse by the Earl of Lauderdale in 1668.

THE QUEEN'S LOBBY

PICTURES

11 Adriaen Hanneman: *William Hamilton, Earl of Lanark and 2nd Duke of Hamilton*, 1650.

THE LESSER APARTMENTS

Access to these rooms is variable

THE PAGE OF THE BACK STAIRS' ROOM

PICTURES

John Pettie: *Bonnie Prince Charlie entering the Ballroom at Holyroodhouse*, 1892.

Alexis-Simon Belle: *Prince James Francis Edward Stuart*, c. 1700.

Alexis-Simon Belle: *Prince James Francis Edward Stuart with his sister, Princess Louisa Maria Theresa*, 1699.

Alexis-Simon Belle: *Prince James Francis Edward Stuart*.

Anon., Italian School, Roman, eighteenth century: *Henry Benedict Stuart, later Cardinal York*, c. 1760.

THE KING'S WARDROBE

PICTURES

Frederick Elwell: *George V*, 1932.

Attributed to Jean-Baptiste Monnoyer: *Still Life with a Vase of Flowers*, c. 1685 (over door).

Francesco Trevisani: *Prince James Francis Edward Stuart*, 1719.

Anon., British School, eighteenth century: *An Incident in the Rebellion of 1745*, c. 1745-50.

THE KING'S DRESSING ROOM

PICTURES

David Jagger: *Queen Mary*, 1929-30.

THE COLLISION of the remains of the Abbey with the rearing bulk of the Palace demonstrates how the original religious foundation was subsumed by the royal residence. Only the nave of the Abbey Church has survived.

The Church must have been begun soon after its foundation by David I in 1128. The processional door leading from the cloisters is the sole surviving feature of c. 1195-1230. The original church was replaced by a cathedral-scaled building. This was built around the existing walls, enabling the Church to continue in use until most of the new design was in place, when the early work was demolished. The interior of the north wall of the nave was given distinctive interlaced arcades but the style changed as work advanced. The west front was richly articulated around the deeply recessed and highly ornamented west door. To create an impressive frontage facing Edinburgh, the width of the west façade was increased by two large square towers (one later engrossed by the Palace). The vaulting over the nave in stone shows the ambition of the builders; but only the southern-most line of vaulting survived the collapse of the roof in 1768.

Possibly because of instability, Abbot Crawford (1460–83) added the flying buttresses. In the 'Rough-Wooing' raid of 1544, Sir Richard Lee looted the lectern (now at the Church of St Stephen, St Albans, Herts). The Nave owes its survival to its adoption as the parish church for the burghs of the Canongate. The remains of the eastern portions of the Abbey were cleared c. 1570. The Church was patched up in 1633 for Charles I's coronation when the decorative reticulated tracery was introduced into the east window and the upper zone of the west front was embellished in a contemporary style.

The Abbey attracted many burials including those of several Scottish kings and members of the Royal Family. Such of their remains as could be rescued from the various phases of destruction are now interred in the royal vault which is surrounded by many handsome monuments.

THE GARDENS are dramatically overshadowed by the towering crags of Arthur's Seat, and encircled by the Queen's Park, which brings an extensive acreage of countryside into the heart of the city. The bleakness of the gardens caused by late-Georgian and Victorian attempts to improve the Palace's amenity has now been transformed by the growth of screens of trees introduced to hide the scars of industry. The Prince Consort is said to have taken a particular interest in the schemes for the gardens. The most ingenious feature of their design is the way in which the garden wall to the south-east is banked up with earth in a form of ha-ha, which, by concealing the boundaries, gives the impression that the gardens flow into the park.

Sadly the new northern approach in 1856 sacrificed the walled Privy

Garden to the north of the Forecourt. Its two surviving relics are what was fancifully known as Mary Queen of Scots' sundial – actually designed and carved by John Mylne in 1633 – and Queen Mary's Bath (now isolated from the gardens), which may be a sixteenth-century garden building but whose true history remains unclear.

A garden party is held each year during the Queen's visit to the Palace of Holyroodhouse in July.

West door of the Abbey

Published by Michael Joseph Limited in association with Royal Collection Enterprises Limited

Penguin Books Limited
27 Wrights Lane, London W8 5TZ

No part of this publication may be reproduced by any means without the permission of Michael Joseph Limited and the copyright holder.

Text written by Ian Gow
Copyright © 1995 Royal Collection Enterprises Limited

Illustrations: all copyright © Her Majesty The Queen, except those on pages 2, 4, 5 and 23, copyright: Royal Commission on the Ancient and Historical Monuments of Scotland

Colour reproduction by Saxon Photolitho, Norwich

Printed in Great Britain by
Butler & Tanner Ltd,
Frome and London

A catalogue record for this book is available from the British Library

ISBN: 0 7181 3967 4

Acknowledgements:
Anne Askwith, Alec Cobbe, Kitty Cruft, John G. Dunbar, Dr Richard Fawcett, John Gifford, Fiona Jamieson, Iain McIvor, Dr Rosalind Marshall, Veronica Steele, Margaret Swain, Donald Wickes